Great Artists

Vincent Van Gogh

ABDO
Publishing Company

Adam G. Klein

visit us at
www.abdopublishing.com

Published by ABDO Publishing Company, 4940 Viking Drive, Edina, Minnesota 55435.
Copyright © 2007 by Abdo Consulting Group, Inc. International copyrights reserved in all
countries. No part of this book may be reproduced in any form without written permission from
the publisher. The Checkerboard Library™ is a trademark and logo of ABDO Publishing
Company.

Printed in the United States.

Cover Photo: Bridgeman Art Library
Interior Photos: Art Resource pp. 11, 13, 19, 27; Bridgeman Art Library pp. 1, 9, 13, 15, 25;
    Corbis pp. 5, 8, 21, 29; Getty Images pp. 4, 17, 23

Series Coordinator: Megan M. Gunderson
Editors: Megan M. Gunderson, Megan Murphy
Cover Design: Neil Klinepier
Interior Design: Dave Bullen

Library of Congress Cataloging-in-Publication Data

Klein, Adam G., 1976-
  Vincent van Gogh / Adam G. Klein.
    p. cm. -- (Great artists)
  Includes index.
  ISBN-10 1-59679-730-4
  ISBN-13 978-1-59679-730-7
  1. Gogh, Vincent van, 1853-1890--Juvenile literature. 2. Painters--Netherlands--Biography--
Juvenile literature. I. Gogh, Vincent van, 1853-1890. II. Title III. Series: Klein, Adam G.,
1976- . Great artists.

  ND653.G7K495 2006
  759.9492--dc22
                                                                          2005017897

Contents

Vincent van Gogh

Vincent van Gogh is considered one of the greatest Dutch painters. He is also among the most important Postimpressionists. However, Van Gogh often felt sad and alone. Through his use of color and distinctive brushstrokes, Van Gogh's artwork reflects the strong emotions he felt.

Although he was sometimes depressed, Van Gogh was also enthusiastic about many things. He created works based on themes that interested him. These themes include peasant life, self-portraits, and scenes from nature.

Van Gogh painted for only ten years. In that time, he completed more than 800 oil paintings and 700 drawings. Only one of Van Gogh's paintings sold while he was alive. But after he died, many people were drawn to his works. Today, Van Gogh's art remains extremely popular.

In 1889, Van Gogh painted **Portrait of the Artist Without His Beard.**

Van Gogh's homes were another common theme in his work. In 1889, Van Gogh painted Vincent's Bedroom in Arles. Portrait of the Artist Without His Beard *appears above the bed.*

Timeline

1853 ~ On March 30, Vincent Willem van Gogh was born in Zundert, Netherlands.

1869 to 1876 ~ Van Gogh worked for Goupil & Co. in the Netherlands, England, and France.

1883 ~ Van Gogh moved to Drenthe to paint landscapes.

1884 ~ Van Gogh painted a series of 40 peasant heads.

1885 ~ Van Gogh painted *The Potato Eaters* and *Still Life with Three Birds' Nests*.

1886 ~ Van Gogh studied at the École des Beaux-Arts in Antwerp, Belgium.

1888 ~ Van Gogh painted *The Café Terrace on the Place du Forum, Arles, at Night* and *The Night Café in the Place Lamartine in Arles*; in December, Van Gogh cut off part of his ear and was hospitalized.

1889 ~ Van Gogh painted 150 paintings in Saint-Rémy-de-Provence, France, including *Starry Night*.

1890 ~ *The Red Vineyard* sold; on July 29, Van Gogh died in Auvers-sur-Oise, France.

Fun Facts

- Vincent van Gogh was named after his grandfather and his uncle Cent. Van Gogh's brother Theo and his wife named their son Vincent, too.

- Van Gogh's art teacher in Tilburg, Netherlands, influenced his artistic life. Constantijn Huysmans shared with Van Gogh the importance of making copies of works by other artists. And, Huysmans believed in the importance of observing nature. Van Gogh did both of these things throughout his short career.

- In 1872, Vincent and Theo began writing letters to one another. This would continue for nearly 18 years.

- Van Gogh abandoned a large number of works when he left the Drenthe region. At first, they remained in his room at the inn where he had stayed. But when the innkeepers realized he wasn't coming back, they began giving away his paintings as gifts! And later, when they needed to use the room again, they burned the remaining works one by one in the stove.

Growing Up

Vincent Willem van Gogh was born on March 30, 1853, in Zundert, Netherlands. Vincent's father, Theodorus van Gogh, was a pastor. Vincent's mother was named Anna Cornelia Carbentus. She was from The Hague, which was a **cultural** center in the Netherlands.

There were six Van Gogh children. Vincent was the oldest, followed by Anna, Theo, Elisabeth, Willemina, and Cornelis. Vincent had an especially close relationship with his younger brother Theo. They were only four years apart in age.

As a child, Vincent loved reading. He also enjoyed being in nature. His favorite outdoor activities included collecting insects and studying plants and animals.

Van Gogh lived in this house in Zundert, Netherlands.

Beginning in 1861, Vincent attended the village school in Zundert. At age 11, he transferred to a boarding school in a neighboring town. Later, he went to a school in Tilburg, Netherlands. There, he studied French, German, English, and mathematics. But most important, Vincent was able to study art. Art interested Vincent because he came from a family of art dealers.

Van Gogh's love of nature continued throughout his life. His sunflower paintings became some of his most famous works.

Off to Work

In 1869, Vincent was **apprenticed** to Goupil & Co. as an art dealer. The company had offices in several European cities. Vincent worked in The Hague. And in 1873, his brother Theo joined Goupil & Co.'s office in Brussels, Belgium.

In May 1873, Goupil & Co. transferred Vincent to London, England. That fall, Theo took a position at the office in The Hague. Then in 1875, Vincent transferred to Paris, France.

Vincent's work with Goupil & Co. helped him learn to appreciate art. In each city, he was exposed to new museums and artists. Vincent enjoyed looking at the works of Rembrandt, as well as other Dutch masters. His favorite artists also included French painters Jean-François Millet and Camille Corot.

Vincent was learning a lot about art, but he no longer liked his job. In early 1876, he was dismissed from Goupil & Co. He returned to England and got a job as an assistant preacher. Vincent delivered his first sermon in November 1876.

Early Influence

While working for Goupil & Co., Van Gogh came into contact with the works of many important artists. Goupil & Co. sold original art by new artists and reproductions by established artists. Part of Van Gogh's job was to distribute these works. As he was exposed to works by more artists, he began to form his own opinions about the styles he preferred.

Van Gogh enjoyed the work of Camille Corot, who was famous for his landscapes. Van Gogh was also introduced to work by The Hague School. This group of artists became known for their scenes of outdoor and daily life. In London, Van Gogh studied both English landscapes and scenes of people in everyday city settings. His interest in these subjects would continue when he began painting seriously later in life.

Van Gogh painted Thatched Cottages in Cordeville *in the theme of The Hague School.*

Peasants

As a pastor himself, Vincent's father insisted that Vincent be properly educated to do this work. However, Vincent decided he did not need formal studies. Instead, he went to a training school in Brussels for a short time. In late 1878, Vincent got a job as a **missionary**. He was sent to the Borinage, a Belgian mining region.

Vincent was a missionary during the **Industrial Revolution**. At that time, fewer people were working in farming. More were taking manufacturing jobs. They worked in dangerous conditions for little money. Life was difficult for peasants living in the Borinage.

Vincent wanted to help the peasants. At one point, he gave away all of his possessions in order to help the poorest coal miners. Because of this, the church thought that his religious practices were becoming too extreme. So, Vincent was removed from his post.

After leaving the Borinage, Van Gogh created many peasant-themed paintings. He was inspired by Jean-François Millet's The Sower *(left). Van Gogh painted his own version of the work several times, including this later work* (right).

Vincent became discouraged about what he was meant to be doing with his life. A former teacher encouraged him to stay in the Borinage and try artwork again. So, he lived among the peasants and drew them. When Vincent went back to drawing, his self-esteem began to return.

Hard Work

Despite his interest in art, Van Gogh had very little training. So at first, his figures were stiff. He also had difficulty with proportion. And, he struggled with **perspective**.

In 1880, Van Gogh left the Borinage. He went to Brussels, where he briefly studied drawing at the Brussels Academy. In 1881, he moved in with his parents in Etten, Netherlands.

During this time, Van Gogh fell in love with a woman named Kee Vos-Stricker. But, Van Gogh's family did not approve of the match. This pushed him away from his family. And, Vos-Stricker did not return his feelings.

At the same time, Anton Mauve was working nearby in The Hague. Mauve was a Dutch landscape painter and related to Van Gogh. Van Gogh visited Mauve, and the artist taught him about **watercolors**. Mauve also gave Van Gogh helpful criticism of his work.

In The Hague, Van Gogh obtained a perspective frame.
He said using this tool was like looking through a window.
It helped him paint increasingly challenging scenes.

Meanwhile, Van Gogh's ideas about religion were changing. So, he argued a lot with his father. When his father asked him to leave, Van Gogh moved to The Hague. There, he could be closer to Mauve.

The Hague

In 1882, Van Gogh rented a studio in The Hague. He took art classes and met many artists. He also had more lessons with Mauve. And that summer, Van Gogh experimented with oil painting.

During this time, Van Gogh met a woman named Sien. She and several of her family members were his models. Eventually, Van Gogh took in Sien and her daughter. His friends and family did not like the arrangement, but Van Gogh wanted to help Sien.

Luckily, some people still supported Van Gogh. His uncle Cornelis **commissioned** 12 views of The Hague. Van Gogh also received money from Theo. But, he used most of it for paints and **canvases**. So, there was not enough money to support himself and Sien. Eventually, the two drifted apart.

In 1883, Van Gogh moved from The Hague to Drenthe to be surrounded by nature. Drenthe was a region of the northern

Beach at Scheveningen in Stormy Weather (above) *is one of Van Gogh's earliest oil paintings. Van Gogh's new interest in painting allowed him to express himself with color. Later, he would become known for his distinctive use of color and thick paint.*

Netherlands that had not been changed as much by the **Industrial Revolution**. There, Van Gogh painted landscapes. But, he soon became lonely in this solitary region.

The Potato Eaters

In December 1883, Van Gogh returned to live with his parents. They were now living in Nuenen, Netherlands. At first, Van Gogh's relationship with his parents remained tense. But soon after he arrived, Van Gogh's mother broke her leg. Van Gogh cared for her, which his father appreciated. So, their relationship improved.

The quality of Van Gogh's work continued to progress quickly. In Nuenen, he drew and painted the weavers of the area. Van Gogh also decided to focus once again on painting peasant life. And in 1884, he created a series of 40 peasant heads. These peasant studies led to one of Van Gogh's early masterpieces, *The Potato Eaters*, from 1885.

While in Nuenen, Van Gogh began having trouble finding models. So in 1885, he painted **still lifes** such as *Still Life with Three Birds' Nests*. Soon, Van Gogh was ready for city life again. In November of that year, he left the Netherlands for the last time.

Artist's Corner

Vincent van Gogh

In the mid-1880s, Van Gogh's artistic style began to emerge. He used colors to set the mood of a work. Whether bright or dark, the colors were chosen specifically to reflect the setting and feel of a scene.

The Potato Eaters (below) is one of Van Gogh's first large works. In this painting, he used dark colors. Van Gogh even mixed primary colors together to create gray.

Along with dark colors, Van Gogh used texture to create emotion. He used choppy brushwork and applied thick, uneven paint. Van Gogh said that "sometimes the material, the nature of things themselves requires thick paint." With *The Potato Eaters*, he wanted to make his figures look as if they were painted with the very earth they worked.

Van Gogh moved from the Netherlands to Antwerp, Belgium. At the beginning of 1886, he spent two months studying there at the École des Beaux-Arts. But, Van Gogh still preferred to teach himself art. So in 1886, he moved to Paris.

Van Gogh had never seen Impressionist artwork before. Theo had tried to describe it to him. But, Van Gogh could not picture it until he saw it for himself in Paris. Van Gogh liked the bright colors the Impressionists used. And, he was thrilled by their short, expressive brushstrokes. He was especially interested in a style called **Pointillism**.

Van Gogh and several French artists of the time borrowed elements from the Impressionists. For example, Van Gogh adopted their use of brilliant colors. But instead of just using short brushstrokes, he also painted short, bright lines of color. The new style was later called Postimpressionism.

In Paris, Van Gogh began using the bold, contrasting colors and strong outlines typical of Japanese prints (right) *in his own work* (left).

Paris was a great city for artists. There, Van Gogh painted more than 20 self-portraits. And, a few of his works were displayed in the window of a paint shop. Van Gogh also organized an exhibition at a local restaurant for himself and his friends. But Van Gogh's life in Paris was tiring. On February 19, 1888, he left Paris for Arles, a city in southern France near the Mediterranean Sea.

The Yellow House

    Van Gogh's studio in Arles was called the "Yellow House." Originally, he envisioned the studio as an open place where artists could come to freely share ideas and resources. He wanted the Yellow House to become a place where he and his friends could live and work together.

    Van Gogh's time in Arles was very productive. He painted two of his most famous works there. One was *The Café Terrace on the Place du Forum, Arles, at Night.* The other was *The Night Café in the Place Lamartine in Arles.* Van Gogh completed both in 1888.

    Meanwhile, Postimpressionist Paul Gauguin was having financial troubles. Together, Van Gogh and Theo convinced him to move into the Yellow House. In honor of his arrival, Van Gogh filled Gauguin's room with a series of sunflower paintings.

Van Gogh and Gauguin both had strong personalities. They often disagreed, which led to arguments. After one of these fights, Van Gogh performed one of his most famous acts. On December 24, 1888, Van Gogh cut off the lower half of his left ear.

Van Gogh enjoyed painting night scenes such as **The Café Terrace on the Place du Forum, Arles, at Night** *.*

Starry Night

After the incident, Van Gogh was hospitalized. Two weeks later, he returned to the Yellow House. But, Gauguin had left. And to make matters worse, Theo planned to marry in the spring. Van Gogh felt abandoned.

In February 1889, Van Gogh was hospitalized again in Arles. But, he was allowed outside during the day to paint. In May, Van Gogh moved to a nearby **psychiatric** institution in Saint-Rémy-de-Provence. There, he created 150 paintings in just one year.

At the **asylum**, Van Gogh could come and go with his doctor's permission. During the day, Van Gogh spent time in the nearby fields painting flowers or trees. Asylum rules kept him indoors at night. So, he painted some night scenes from memory, including *Starry Night*. Theo said these were some of the most beautiful works of his brother's career. Later, **critics** agreed.

Opposite page: Starry Night

Auvers-sur-Oise

Eventually, Van Gogh left the **asylum** at Saint-Rémy-de-Provence. He went to Paris to see Theo. Soon, the time and effort he had devoted to his work at Saint-Rémy-de-Provence began to pay off. In 1890, his painting *The Red Vineyard* sold for 400 Belgian francs.

Around this time, Van Gogh's work was also included in several art shows. Two works were exhibited at the Salon des Indépendents in 1889, followed by ten in 1890. That same year, six works were shown at a Les Vingt exhibition. Even Gauguin praised Van Gogh's recent works.

However, Paris was too loud and crowded for Van Gogh. So, he went to live in Auvers-sur-Oise. The town was near Paris, so he would still be close to Theo. And in Auvers-sur-Oise, Van Gogh could be treated by a physician and painter named Dr. Paul-Ferdinand Gachet.

Dr. Gachet encouraged Van Gogh to forget about his illness and focus on painting. Van Gogh followed his advice and completed

Van Gogh painted The Red Vineyard *in 1888.*
Two years later, it was shown at the Les Vingt exhibition.

nearly one painting each day. Still, Van Gogh's illness overcame him. And on July 29, 1890, he died from a **self-inflicted** gunshot wound.

More Appreciation

Many of Van Gogh's friends attended his funeral. His coffin was draped in sunflowers. And his **easel**, stool, and brushes were set nearby. Van Gogh was buried on a hill in Auvers-sur-Oise.

When Theo died six months later, his wife inherited all of Van Gogh's works. Today, most of these works are part of the collection of the Van Gogh Museum in Amsterdam, Netherlands.

Van Gogh's work reflects his life and has inspired many artists after him. But, only after his death did people appreciate his talent. Van Gogh's artwork remains incredibly popular today. On November 19, 1998, Van Gogh's *Portrait of the Artist Without His Beard* sold for $71 million. It was one of the highest prices ever paid for a painting.

Opposite page: *Van Gogh's work influenced future art movements such as Fauvism. The Fauvists used bold colors, expressive brushstrokes, and thick paint. Sometimes they applied the paint directly from the tube to the canvas!*

Glossary

apprentice - a person who learns a trade or a craft from a skilled worker.

asylum - an institution that protects and cares for those in need, especially the mentally ill, the poor, or orphans.

canvas - a piece of cloth that is framed and used as a surface for a painting.

commission - a request to complete a work, such as a painting, for a certain person. To be commissioned is to be given such a request.

critic - a professional who gives his or her opinion on art or performances.

culture - the customs, arts, and tools of a nation or people at a certain time.

easel - a stand that holds a painter's canvas.

Industrial Revolution - the period in the 1800s when new machinery and technology changed the world economy.

missionary - a person who spreads a church's religion.

perspective - the art of giving objects drawn on a flat surface the illusion of being three-dimensional.

Pointillism - the use of small brushstrokes and small dots of color so that they blend together when seen from a distance.

psychiatric - of or relating to a branch of medicine that identifies and treats mental, emotional, or behavioral illnesses.

self-inflicted - of or relating to something caused and endured by oneself.

still life - a painting or a picture made up of nonmoving objects.

watercolor - a paint made by mixing dye with water.

Saying It

Arles - AWRL
Borinage - baw-ree-NAHZH
École des Beaux-Arts - ay-KAWL day boh-ZAHR
Paul Gauguin - pawl goh-gan
Saint-Rémy-de-Provence - sehn-ray-mee-duh-praw-VAHNS

Web Sites

To learn more about Vincent van Gogh, visit ABDO Publishing Company on the World Wide Web at **www.abdopublishing.com**. Web sites about Van Gogh are featured on our Book Links page. These links are routinely monitored and updated to provide the most current information available.

Index